Bullies to Buddies

Andres Maeso

Written By Andres D. Maeso
Illustrations by Andres D. Maeso and Irina Flowers

Layout and Design by: BYSTANDUP

Text Copyright ©2011 by Andres D. Maeso
Illustrations Copyright© 2013 by Andres D. Maeso

No part of this publication may be reproduced in whole or part or stored in a retrieval system, or transmitted in any form or by any means, electronic, mechanical, photocopying, recording, or otherwise without the written permission of the author.

ISBN 978-0-615-95873-6

www.bystandup.com

Jake laughs at Billy after he trips him and pushes him to the ground.

"Hahaha"

All of the team leaves to go home while Billy is still sitting on the ground and he starts crying.

The next day Billy wakes up really sad. He stomps down the stairs and starts eating his cereal. He does not talk to his mom.

His mom asks "Honey, what's wrong? Is everything ok?"

Billy says "Everything is fine" because he does not want to talk about it.

Even though he would rather skip it,
he goes outside to go to soccer practice.

Jake jumps out from behind a bush and takes Billy's soccer bag. He throws it in the trash, then he runs away.

Billy has to climb into the trashcan full of yucky stuff to get his bag. Then he runs because he is late for practice.

When he gets to practice everyone on the team laughs at him because he is so dirty.

The coach pulls him aside and asks him:

"What's going on Billy?
You look upset!"

Billy says with his voice shaking,

"Jake is picking on me. He trips me, makes fun of me and took my bag and threw it in the trashcan!"

"Well Billy, looks like we are dealing with a bully."

"We need to find a way to make the bully your buddy."

"Here is what we will do"
    and he whispers into Billy's ear.

"BULLY TO BUDDY"

Billy goes back on the soccer field and the coach says, "Everyone will teach each other today."

"I will select who your buddy will be."

Billy thinks *"Bully to Buddy!"*

Billy's buddy is Jake.

Billy teaches Jake two new soccer moves so he can become a better player.

The coach watches as Jake tries the moves and is happy.

The coach thinks "Bullies to Buddies"

The next day they have a game and Jake scores a goal using the new moves Billy taught him.

Everyone cheers and Jake goes over to Billy, smiles and says:

"Thanks Buddy!"

Billy smiles as he's thinking "Bullies to Buddies!"

About the Author

Andres Maeso, known to his friends as Andrew resides in Williamsburg, Virginia. He wrote this book when he was in middle school.

The inspiration for the book was experiencing bullying firsthand and seeing other kids being bullied. Andrew is an honor student and holds several offices in his high school.

Andrew has been playing soccer since he was four years old. He plays soccer at the varsity, state, and premier levels. In addition to playing soccer, Andrew teaches soccer classes, coaches and referees young children ranging in ages from two to nine.

He wants to give back to his community the love of the game! He has made it his practice to assist others and hopes this book will help young children to seek help from others when needed.

BYSTANDUP: an anti-bullying resource for teachers, counselors, school administrators, community leaders, parents, & students.

Visit www.bystandup.com for more information.

www.ingramcontent.com/pod-product-compliance
Lightning Source LLC
Chambersburg PA
CBHW041542040426
42446CB00002B/205